THE SPACE BETWEEN US

THE SPACE BETWEEN US

Courtney Peppernell
Zack Grey

Andrews McMeel
PUBLISHING®

Acknowledgments

We wanted to dedicate this book to any person in a long-distance relationship or friendship. We have both had experience with such relationships and the longing and ache that comes along with them. We wanted to thank every person who has assisted with the creation of this collaboration, including James, Pepperbooks, Andrews McMeel Universal, and our families.

Soon . . .

It will be hello,
I've missed
you.
I'm so glad
you're home.

Soon,
you won't be there.
Instead, you'll be here,
and all the aching moments
I haven't had your hand
calmly sitting in mine
will all but disappear
as our fingers entwine.

Soon,
my lips won't ache,
craving the way you taste.
My body will mold itself
so perfectly into yours,
my heart will skip a million times
just by the look in your eyes.

Soon,
I will probably cry
the moment you arrive,
just like I did the first time.
It fills me with happiness
to know you are all mine.

Soon,
we will wake up each morning,
reach to the other side of the bed,
and hold each other so closely.
There will be no need for
good-morning texts to be read.

Soon,
I will whisper to you,
"You are forever the name
stitched into my heart,"
all day, every day
(all night, every night).

Soon,
I will spend all my moments
wrapped up in you
to make memories we'll keep,
so that the next time we are apart,
I'll think of all those moments
when it's too hard to sleep.

Soon . . .
your hand won't be so far;
your lips won't be miles away.
Our hearts will connect
all the space between us,
and with me you will stay.

for those whose love knows no bounds

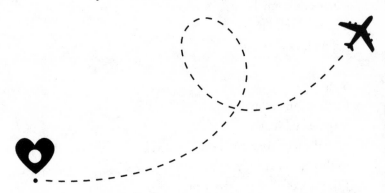

Destinations

At First Glance

Before you, I never counted seconds, or minutes, or hours. Before you, I never understood how feelings could find their way into text messages or long, drawn-out phone calls. Before you, I never smiled so hard every time a name appeared on my phone or felt my heart beat so fast the moment a face lit up my screen. Before you, I never knew how love could be measured by all the miles in between.

Courtney Peppernell

pictures,

sound,
the collision.

saw you,
called you,
watched you move.

even from the first time
i looked into your eyes,
the reality was better

than i ever
could have
imagined.

Zack Grey

Here we are,
just two stars,
floating in the universe
with what feels like
light-years between us.

A handful of conversations
either side of the moon,
but I adore every moment
I get to speak with you.

How I wish the stars
would collide,
and into your arms I would fall,
unraveled by the way you smile,
like I've never been in love before.

Courtney Peppernell

you weren't the only one;
the only name on my screen,
the only pretty girl charmed by
pretty words.

but i never knew if you were
coming or going,
building or destroying,
living or dying.

you were something beautiful
in ways that the eyes can't see.
you were a poem before you
met the poet,
a story before there were
words to tell it.

you were a surprise
to a clairvoyant,
the voice
of a mime,
colors to the blind.

everyone else met my
low expectations,
but you—

you made me
believe in magic.

Zack Grey

So, I've added your time zone to my phone, and I check the weather where you are in my spare time. I've favorited your number; I nearly know it by heart. I have your picture as my wallpaper, and I'm daydreaming about your hand in mine. I hope when I finally see you, your soul will come alive. I hope in the meantime, you see my face in your dreams. I just can't wait until you arrive.

Courtney Peppernell

when my
screen
lights up
with your
name,
so do i.

Zack Grey

When I think of you, I imagine us as two hearts destined to find each other. I am lost in the way I miss you but not lost in the way I feel for you. I crave you, the sweetness of your voice, the softness of your touch, the kindness of your heart. But my heart doesn't know distance. I can love you from two thousand miles away as easily as I can love you if I saw you every day.

you sent me hearts
(your heart)
you gave me likes
(you liked me)

& for once
the meaningless
feedback loop
of internet approval

meant
so
much
more.

Zack Grey

There is a road by my house, cut off from the highway. A road once traveled, now lonely, forgotten. I wish I could turn back time, find the lines stitching the roads together, hold them there, keep them from unraveling. Like the lonely road, I miss you. I feel threads of my soul as they pull apart. I just want to kiss your lips, your forehead, your hands, your thighs, your back. I just want to kiss you all over and remind you how much you mean to me. How much I believe our love is stronger than the forgotten roads that keep us from each other.

Courtney Peppernell

i wasn't the only one.

(a girl like you never
shows her cards too soon.)

but we both knew it
right from the beginning;

i am the king
to your queen.

Sitting in front of the mirror getting ready for a night out is never the same without you here. I just want to stay in, curl up with you in bed. Rather than sitting in the same old bar, watching my friends, thinking about you instead. I knew the moment I first saw you this would be more than just a little crush, because it's a mystery to me how you are miles away but you somehow make my blood rush.

I wish we were under the same sky
But your skies shine gold
while mine are gray and rainy and bold
I look to the moon at night
hoping she will send a message to you
whispering my love across the sea
the light holding on to you

i've never seen happiness
but i've seen your face
and i cannot find
the difference

Zack Grey

She can't kiss me each night or unbutton my blouse; she can't hold me when the dust has settled after each fight. But she sends me long texts and we talk every morning, how in the beginning I wasn't sure if the distance could work, but my heart is sure, and she says that's all that matters. One day, we will get to spend dawn to dusk together, and when I reach across the covers for her, she will be more than what I have dreamt into existence; she will be with me, and we'll finally be free of this distance.

Courtney Peppernell

We started to learn things about each other from the inside out, like the summer you broke your ankle and how for every birthday you just wanted ice-cream cake. Even if I started to imagine the taste of your skin on my lips, the rhythm of every beat of your heart, the way your body would fit in mine, I was amazed at the way we could find beauty just in each other's energy. I had been introduced to the very seams that stitched you together. Before I knew every line on your body, the color of your eyes, the touch of your hand, I knew the folds of your heart, your stories, your soul, and nothing compared. Part of me wondered if this was what love truly was, that even if I had my eyes closed for the rest of my life, I would still fall for you anyway.

I'm thinking about a beautiful girl and her eyes that remind me of stardust settled across a deep-blue sky. I am thinking about a beautiful girl and how I want to buy her coffee and plan dates to museums, cinemas, and libraries. I am thinking about a beautiful girl whose voice takes my breath away every time, how all I want to do is listen to her day over cheese and wine. I am thinking about a beautiful girl whom I would kiss every day, every hour, forever and ever, if only she didn't live so many miles away. I am thinking about a beautiful girl who deserves the whole universe, how just knowing her makes my heart burst.

Courtney Peppernell

i met your smile
over the counter of
a busy café
in venice.

i met your smile
from across a
rushing
japanese river.

i met your smile
from a hospital bed
(and it healed me
like medicine never could).

this time, i met your smile
through a screen
thousands of miles
apart from you.

but what i'm saying is,
maybe—just maybe—
it wasn't the first time.

(& i hope it's not the last)

Zack Grey

That was when I finally
knew how I felt for you.
When I didn't just miss you
in the moments I was alone.
I missed you
even when I had things to do.
And all I could think about
was how I was apart from you.

you were a cold rain
on a hot summer day:

unexpected
but very welcome.

Zack Grey

My friends say
I should just
let you go,
because all this
waiting
isn't good
for my soul.

But if they
only knew
how you light up
my heart even if
we're so far apart.

If they only knew
how perfect
we are together,
they'd know
this love is
just like any other.

Courtney Peppernell

There are only so many words I can fit in a text message or an email or a love letter. There are only so many times I can call you throughout the day. There are only so many sweaters you can send me, so that I can have a small piece of you here. Instead of being wrapped up in your arms, you tell me about the dog that lives on your corner, how he comes to the fence to greet you each day. Instead of pressing your lips to my knuckles, you tell me about the flowers growing in your garden, how they are now covering the archway. Instead of planning our lazy weekend and what we may do, you tell me about airfares and train tickets and how we just have to wait a little longer, and then I will have you.

Courtney Peppernell

you deserve
every star
to shine for you
the way my eyes do

Zack Grey

There I was, with an almond latte, scribbling in a notebook, and you sent me a message, so different from all the others. Maybe it was more about how I felt this need to reply or that the smile in all your pictures caught my eye. Now I'm wondering what your lips taste like and how your skin feels against mine. I fall asleep to the sound of your voice, recorded messages I play on repeat. You make me feel like I exist just to know you, as though the universe gave us no other choice.

sometimes i wonder
why i held on to you
when i was so used to
people coming and going
like the tide.

maybe it's the way you entered.
you were a wave without
the whitecaps.
an ocean that let me
wade in slowly.

Zack Grey

I know you just want to be seen, to have someone listen to you, support you, grow with you. I don't care about the time zones or the late calls, or that you begin your day when I'm coming home. I don't care about the distance or the ocean in between. I only care about you. I see you without ever having *seen* you.

there's a homeless lady
sitting in the corner
at the coffee shop.

it's the middle of winter,
and she's smiling to herself
like she finally feels at home.

i think you must be my coffee shop.
my break from wandering
outside in the cold.

(the home i've been looking for all along.)

Zack Grey

The timing of life
had a funny way of
swiping right,
and suddenly
I'm thinking of a girl
across the bay,
too many miles away,
and yet
I'm spending nights
dancing in LA.

Courtney Peppernell

you make me
want to
touch the stars
play connect the dots
hello constellation
trail kisses in space
you make me
want to
love your face

Zack Grey

Sometimes you find someone, and it doesn't matter that they live a world away or they count stars while you go about your day; you just know that, above everything, you were meant to find each other. It's so beautifully honest that you fit together; that you make each other better; that no matter where they are or where you are, they help you to build a life. Suddenly, in all this chaos, you have found something to hold on to. This beautiful person, miles and miles away, has made you realize how much you can love someone without ever really meeting.

I've never been a morning person,
but now I wake up before the sunrise
just to sit on the phone with you
while you watch your sunset.

Courtney Peppernell

you taught my
smile to be brighter
just by seeing yours

Zack Grey

Distant and Young

My friends are tired of the way I miss you, and my parents don't understand. My teachers ask what is wrong, but no one gets it like you can. My love lives miles away, and we're too broke for plane and train tickets. But I have hope I will see you someday, because the color of your eyes is my new favorite, and making mixtapes of our songs makes me feel better. Every road, no matter the distance, leads me back to you.

Courtney Peppernell

33

Who knew that my heart
could beat so fast
from just a text or a photo of you,
or a long update about
what happened in your week.
I am hanging off every part
you share with me,
every little word you say.

Courtney Peppernell

i'm not afraid of love,
just cautious of reckless people;

tell me, darling,
do you like to

crash cars &
watch them burn

or save a survivor
with the jaws of life?

Zack Grey

It was July, the first time we met. It was such a hot summer night, so we sat on the roof of your car, parked out by the beach. You had me wrapped in your arms, music playing from your phone, and you told me you didn't want to go back home. So, I asked if you believed in more than one lifetime and said I knew I had always been yours. The distance will never matter if we find each other in every year. We can bear the time apart if we fiercely love each other in the time we are together.

Courtney Peppernell

i will hand you
every piece of me
down to these very bones
if you just smile like that
one more time

Zack Grey

It's the little things I notice. How you cancel plans just to call me. The way you remind me how much you care, even if you are far away. When you send me flowers to let me know you are thinking of me. How you never sleep without repairing an argument. The way you try to make me laugh when things seem impossible or the miles unforgivable. How you sent me your sweater so that I would feel closer to you, how you trust me so boldly in everything I do. There are times I don't say it enough, but all those little things don't go unnoticed.

Courtney Peppernell

my human had no clue,
but my soul knew
from the first moment
that you were mine
and always had been.

Zack Grey

We are real, despite what
some people may say.
I am waiting for your whispers
to touch my scars,
and all these aching miles
to turn into inches.

I am waiting for your eyes
on every part of my skin
and my hands to feel
the beat of your heart,
to unearth the moments,
we are yet to begin.

Even if we have started
with so much space between,
you have brought every star to life
with a love that feels like a dream.

Courtney Peppernell

every small decision

was never mine to make.

every step of this unkind journey

led me fatefully back to you—

and it was absolutely, completely

worth it (in every life).

After every long day, the thing that gives me hope is coming home and disappearing into my blankets, waiting for your phone call. How your voice gently tells me the things I long to hear most, even on the nights I feel so lost.

we never wanted
to fit in

we were both
looking for someone
to be different with

Zack Grey

How it makes me happy, the way I roll over in the morning and the connection hasn't dropped out overnight. My heart swells when I can still see her asleep, tangled in her sheets, with messy hair and parted lips. But how it makes me sad that I cannot reach over and awake her with a kiss. My heart drops, knowing I'm going to be without her for weeks and weeks.

i reached for
the stars
& i found
you.

I feel for her soul
and everything she is

Before I had even
touched her skin

Now it's a love
worth holding on to

A love to invest
my whole heart in

Courtney Peppernell

it was beyond your perfect skin—

knowing always is.

i saw you with the eyes

of my soul,

and physical realities

didn't matter anymore.

i knew you were from another

dimension,

and i couldn't wait

to visit.

Zack Grey

We will have every date we've ever wanted, to museums and picnics in the park. Getting drunk at happy hour and stumbling home to bed. We will walk the street holding hands, and all of it won't just be the fantasies in my head.

Living for Tomorrow

All these empty bottles, nights alone trying to drown all these thoughts of you. But it doesn't erase how I'm missing your arms around me or your voice whispering how much you need me. I wish you were here, instead of the pillows I pretend are you. I long for us to be together again.

without you
i'm a whole person
with half a heart

Our sun rises at different times, and it feels like my bags are always packed, ready to board the plane whenever you need me. I just want to enjoy a sunrise with you by my side and not have to think about saying goodbye.

Courtney Peppernell

i was yours
once i closed my eyes
and all i could see
was you
lying next to me

You miss having someone by your side, doing simple things like grocery shopping or driving over late at night. You wish a screen wasn't always in the way and plane tickets weren't so expensive. You just want to have lunch midweek or dinner on a Friday night, or go to the bowling alley when there is nothing else to do. It's even worse when you are having a bad day and all you want is to crawl into their arms and be told everything will be okay. The distance that sits between you will be bearable most times, but sometimes not. But how powerful is a love that says I will be yours no matter the distance?

Courtney Peppernell

they said i'd never make
a life out of words,
and they said
the same thing about you.

thank god
i love nothing
more than
defying expectations.

Zack Grey

We are so far apart, waiting months to share a bed, and yet I still can't imagine sharing nights with anyone else. You are all I think about, a song on repeat in my head.

Courtney Peppernell

i love it when you're silent with me
but my worry sets in
when you're silent at me

Zack Grey

It's only been two minutes
since you hung up the phone,
but it feels like two centuries.

My heart is pounding
louder than any thunderstorm,
reeling from the way you laugh,
a sound I could listen to
for the rest of my life.

You remind me of lightning,
the way you fall from the sky,
so striking, so mesmerizing;
you surge through me.

Courtney Peppernell

don't hang up
not just yet
i'm afraid

the static
from your line
to mine

may never
find the way
back to me

Zack Grey

Our skin is not pressed together, not in the way we danced in sheets through summer, but I still feel the burning in my heart and the touch of your hand. I can't wait to be together again.

you're always in the past
but every time i see your face
it feels like i'm
looking at my future

Zack Grey

Remember how we promised each other to say good morning and hold hands every moment we were together. Remember how we promised to answer when called in the middle of the night. To say "I love you" when the days feel hard to breathe. To remind each other everything will be all right. I think about all our promises, and they make the time worth waiting for. All these memories I want to create with you, if only we lived closer, if only the universe knew how much I just want to be with you.

Courtney Peppernell

you touch your hair
darken your eyes
bite your lip

i know you're thinking this too:

my hand on your back
your lips on my neck
not enough oxygen in the world

when you finally touch me.

Zack Grey

A soul can be split into a thousand pieces and scattered across mountains and rivers and the sea. But my soul, in all its pieces, gathers itself every time we find each other, that's how much you mean to me.

if you were here
i'd put your head
in my lap and
run my hands
through your hair

i'd stop time and tell the birds
"please, be quiet;
my love is resting"

i'd ask the sun to dim
the light of day
and hold the moon
in my hands
till you wake

if you were here
i'd give you magic kisses
to take away the pain

i'd always hold your hand
like it's the first time
and i remember everything

darling, if you were here
i'd show you the world
because you are mine

Zack Grey

Will we make it to the end, will we find all our dreams? The days feel longer sometimes, and we feel further apart. I wonder, if we lived closer, would it be different? But I am still drawn to you, still holding on to your smile, your eyes, your laugh. You are the flame that lights my path.

Courtney Peppernell

i long for the day
when i
touch you in atoms
more than i
see you in pixels

Zack Grey

Tangle your hands
in my hair and kiss me
for as long as the months
we have been apart

Courtney Peppernell

i didn't expect you to be so damn perfect.
why are you so far from me?

what's that on my face?
i've never smiled like this before.

i've been fighting it for a while now,
admitting that i've fallen for you.

you make me happy,
but not happy in a way that feels complete.

more like anticipation.
i can't ignore this anymore;

it feels a lot like love,
but i haven't touched you yet,

felt the softness of your skin
or the heat of your breath on my neck,

seen your coffee eyes
unobstructed by a screen.

what we have is beautiful,
but the truth is,

until i see you,
i'm always living for tomorrow.

Zack Grey

Those weekends we share, laughing quietly to ourselves under the covers, empty pizza boxes all around us. Thinking maybe we should just run away together. I can't stand all the goodbyes or deciding your place or mine; the drive feels longer with every passing highway sign. If life had been a little kinder, perhaps I would have found you in a coffee shop around the corner instead of one out of town, somewhere lonely and so much farther.

you made my
ifs become
whens.
darling,
with you,
i doubt nothing.

The hardest thing about saying goodbye
and watching you leave
is wondering if by missing me
you will only grow your love stronger
or if eventually it will be too much
and be easier just to forget me

Courtney Peppernell

my voice will echo
between mountains
when i tell the world
how i love you

You remind me of honeydew donuts and postcard-type views. You remind me of the kind of love no one ever wants to lose. All these months we wait, and the seas and skies we cross, just to spend a handful of moments together, only to part once more and wait again, is all worth it, as long as it's you walking through that door. Our world beats to its own rhythm, a planet made for you and me and all the hidden messages we share and say. No matter how far the earth is away from the sun, its heart still glows in the same way.

Courtney Peppernell

& this is what we will smell like:

tiger lilies and a hint of vanilla

on your neck;

sandalwood and rose water

on mine.

soon:

sweat,

all over

both of us.

Zack Grey

My memories are sharper, every instance I cling to, because those are the only things I have to hold on to when I am not with you. The first time we met, how you came from the arrival gates and flung into my arms, our first kiss in my car, how we had dreamt about each other's lips for six months. Our first real date, under fairy lights, holding hands, how I had imagined touching your skin, if only once. Now you are across the country again, a face I adore on the other side of my screen, but these memories I hold, engraved in my heart, are the most beautiful that have ever been.

Courtney Peppernell

there's a weight to sleeping alone—

or a lack thereof.

without your body

tethering me to this bed,

i'm always floating away,

at the mercy of

whatever ghosts

haunt my dreams tonight.

Zack Grey

The connection I have with you is stronger than the distance that separates us. The attraction I have to you, deeper than the sea that divides us. This isn't just wanting; you are my soul mate. Now that I've met you, every moment means so much more. How could I possibly take another moment with you for granted again. Not when we have no idea when we will be together again.

i know how to fix everything:

your hand in mine,

a kiss in the rain—

but for now,

there are 1,400 miles

between me and the solution.

Zack Grey

I used to believe that love could only be shared over dinner dates, walks along the sand, or cars parked listening to songs on the radio. But now I know it's found in calls at three in the morning, packages sent with love notes, and dreams of finally seeing each other. For all the things that haunt me, and the baggage I bring, I know that I am safe with you. I know that even without a screen you would still let me in—into your heart, into your home. How you do this, without being right next to me, I still don't even know.

my best reason to smile

every morning:

phone vibrating,

"incoming video call"

(but i can't wait

to wake up to you

without a screen

between your face and mine.)

Zack Grey

I wrote her letters; each are titled a different feeling
    If you are missing me
    If you need a hug
    If you need reminding of our love
    If you feel lonely
And all I really wanted to write was
    If you look outside
And I'd be standing there, my arms wide open
    You'll see me

Courtney Peppernell

sometimes the price
of being the luckiest
man in the world
is being lucky
only half of the time

Zack Grey

Since our love bloomed, I've learned to be more patient. I've learned all this waiting should drive me to be better for us, should make me say the things I'm feeling. We don't need to hurry, we don't need to rush, we will find our way to each other eventually.

i think about kitchen fights;

batter on your nose,

smearing it with my index finger.

i'm covered in flour and you're laughing

because you "didn't think

i could get any whiter."

it is funny,

i'll give you that.

or at least, i will

one day, when we

share the same space

and i'm not just

imagining it.

Zack Grey

I've found my life with you
my passion
my love
What will guide me home to you
are the stars above

yes, i want to be there
when you put the star on
the christmas tree.
i won't fight you for
the opportunity.

i'll laugh about
how short you are
and stand by the ladder
to make sure you're safe.

you'll look at me and smile.
i know it's ordinary. domestic.
boring, even—

but when i'm finally next to you,
i'll be on top. i'll be that star.

(and there's nothing ordinary about that.)

Zack Grey

I would cross every distance for you. The distance from my hand to yours every time we are in the same city, the distance in our sheets to hold you all night long, the distance to walk across a crowded room to reach you. I would cross roads, highways, rivers, and oceans. I would cross eternity, the entire universe, to show you what my love for you is worth.

Courtney Peppernell

i catch myself turning to you.
"two sugars or three?"
as if i'm already
making your coffee
in the mornings.

soon i will look beside me
and the space won't be filled
with a mere imagination of you.
i'll look and
you'll be there.
you will.
soon.

Zack Grey

Thirty years from now, I don't want to regret never telling you how I felt. I don't want to fill the spaces in my heart without ever really knowing what they could look like if they were filled with your name. And I know we are still growing, still becoming ourselves. I know we have miles to go, roads to travel, and storms to weather. I know all of it makes you feel a little overwhelmed. But I will choose you no matter the miles, no matter the roads, no matter the storms.

Courtney Peppernell

i think i scare you sometimes,
the way i talk about the future
like some fixed thing.
like a butterfly wing flapping
deviation in the time line
will throw everything off.
like, oh my god, commitment is scary,
i barely said yes to today,
tomorrow is asking for a lot.
i know. i know i'm overwhelming
and it takes every ancient inch of your soul
to keep your human body from
screaming its way out the door
as i talk about when and how and soon.
i'm sorry i forget, in all my overthinking,
to stop and think about how terrifying it is
to go from *i'm not looking for anything right now*
to *what color should the curtains be?*
i just get a little ahead of myself sometimes.
tomorrow is so much brighter—
it has you in it.

Zack Grey

You feel so close sometimes, and not just a beautiful figure on a screen. It's as though I can feel the warmth of the blanket wrapped around you, smell the scent of your coconut shampoo, taste the coffee by your bedstand. Have I just dreamt you into life, or will we beat these miles and see this love through?

Courtney Peppernell

Lonely Nights

More often than not, I can string words together as though they were lanterns on a page. Lighting the way from my heart to yours. I can speak in sentences the way the moon speaks to the stars. I can write love letters in the way the sun parts the clouds after rain. But how to explain these lonely nights without you, I do not know. You have been in my dreams for so long, sometimes I wonder if I have made you up. You have stolen words from lips, sentences from my heart; you have jumbled my thoughts in such a way I can barely breathe. You have me wondering what it will be like, the moment I can whisper my name into your lips.

i don't miss you
because you're far;

i miss you because
i can feel you near

and my soul has
waited so long

to dance with yours
again.

Zack Grey

She was tired of incomplete love, of connecting and then parting, of promising to explore every inch and barely making the first mile. So, she promised she would focus on herself and grow her own soul for a while.

Courtney Peppernell

the hardest thing about
these lonely nights
isn't your absence;

it's the absence of
any reason to believe
you'll ever be here.

Zack Grey

The world has seen it many times before; it's a lonely story, about how you have feelings for someone you can never have, and you don't know what to do. The narrative isn't clear; the journey seems forgotten. Oh, how I wish you could see the ending clearly, the ending the world already knew. Because it's really just a story about how you survived and realized all that lonely energy was best put into you.

i'm looking at the stars
but i'm thinking of you

Zack Grey

For so long, I have been growing apart from my soul. Not knowing which road to take or which way to go. Every time I look to the sky, I wonder where it will guide me, what it will tell me to do. I wonder, when I look up, do you look up too? I am slowly admitting that old wounds are still open, and if I am to ever come home to myself, I need to walk the road alone.

lately i've spent a lot of time
sitting quietly in cars

silence feels so empty
without you here

Zack Grey

To pass the time
I've spent so many moments
with the car parked by the river

The radio is on
our favorite song
anything to fill the silence

hold me through
the darkness
and i'll follow you
into the light

Zack Grey

I thought I couldn't do this without you, that I wouldn't survive on my own. But my heart has been so grateful, for every journey, for every thread that has held on. Because my healing and recovery comes from all the parts of me that are so understanding. So, I will remind myself that I deserve to be cared for. If not by someone kind, then most importantly by myself. Laughter is the color of magic and should be embraced each day. My feelings deserve to soar, like birds, free to be expressed. My way back home is my own and not for anyone else to assess.

you're my
3am
wish you were here

Zack Grey

This is just the way life is for me, my phone always charged in case you call, my laptop battery barely alive because I've watched you sleep all night. Making all my plans at the beginning of the week, so I can wait up for you until midnight. It snows where you are, and yet the sun always shines in my hometown. How I would give anything to dance under the snowflakes with you; I'd trade my soul for you to be around.

You wear the night so beautifully.
The moonlight in your hair,
   the stars in your eyes.

But I wear the sun,
and our existence is
   always filled with goodbyes.

Courtney Peppernell

rain drops
all night long

like my stomach
as i begin to doubt

that i'll ever
see you.

Meet me in the folds of your heart, where all our dreams and future plans exist. It is here we will not worry about how many days we've been alone or how many sleepless nights there are to go.

everything is louder
knowing that you exist
but can't be here.
all i can hear is the night
speaking about peace
but not letting me
give myself to it.

Zack Grey

That lonely, aching feeling never made any sense before I met you. Every sad song or sad poem was just a sad song or a sad poem. It never had any meaning. But you and your absence has made me understand. I know why people cry into the pages of books; I know why they place their hands over their hearts every time a sad song plays. Missing you has been like nothing else. A hole in my heart, a sea of sorrow in my soul, all these lonely thoughts in my mind, all the time. I am so in love and yet so alone.

Courtney Peppernell

it's an odd feeling, knowing
you've made it through life
all these years,
mostly unscathed without me,

yet i worry,
knowing that this world
is a prowling beast
that could take you in its claws
at any moment,

and from all the way
over here,
i'd be too late
to save you.

Zack Grey

Your morning falls when it's late at night for me, because you live so far away. I know that there is an ocean between us, a fourteen-hour plane ride just to exist in your space. But I just wanted to say, sometimes I pretend you are here with me. So, in the morning, when I stand in line at the coffee shop, the person in front is really you, because you're ordering my latte too. The car that honks outside is really you, and you're laughing, telling me to get a move on, because we're late for the movies, and this is the one we've been waiting for, for so long. The pillow right next to me is really you, and you're holding me, because someone else broke my heart, and you're the one who puts it back together again, every single part. The missed call about an unpaid bill is really you, calling because you've made dinner reservations at our favorite place to go, to talk all night, until the sun rises through the windowsill. Even if I have to pretend for now and carry you around in my pocket as such, one day I know I will see you again, and I won't have to be so lonely, missing you so much.

—I miss my friends too

Courtney Peppernell

the only thing
that makes these nights
bearable
is the way this promise
flows from your lips:

"soon,
yours will touch mine."

When we got to the bus station, we were forty-five minutes early. I still don't know if it was a blessing or a curse. A blessing because I could spend forty-five minutes more with you or a curse because in those forty-five minutes, I had to watch you cry and beg me not to go. We both knew I had to go, though, because for now our lives are apart, even if we so badly want them to be together. Even if the constant traveling back and forth doesn't feel right anymore, even if staying is all I want to do. The bus arrived, and I felt your hand tighten around mine, a tether between my heart and yours. It doesn't get easier to say goodbye; those words are poison on my lips, and "see you soon" doesn't suffice because we never know how soon "soon" will be. All I have is my love for you, how you light up every deep and dark corner of my soul.

hope is chemotherapy
for the lost—
the same thing
that keeps me holding on
is what's killing me.

Zack Grey

Now we're both lonely,
wishing I was there
or you were here.

And I can't handle all
these minutes, hours, days
we are away from each other.

I'm staring at the ceiling,
in my bed,
wishing I was someplace
with you instead.

Courtney Peppernell

i cannot promise
that you won't cry,
but i can promise
that your tears
will always be
worth it.

Zack Grey

One minute, everything is perfect,
and the next, I need to hear your voice.
I just need to know we'll make it,
that the distance won't break us.

Courtney Peppernell

All this wishing for you to be near, and yet my greatest fear is, what if we don't work when we are closer together? What if our love is only love because we live apart?

i am burning away
when your body is not
lying next to mine.

—*the second law of
thermodynamics*

I ache for you in a way I am scared to share. I feel my body numb from the parts your hands touched, as though they can no longer feel warmth if it is not you. Ghosts of the words we whispered to each other under the dim light of my room haunt me as I try to sleep. And I can only hope that I will see you again soon, before my heart gives out.

Courtney Peppernell

Maybe they call this
"lonely love" for a reason.
How to feel full
when you are not here
to hold me.

How to feel loved
when, instead of arms,
I have only words.

But, oh, how words matter.
How your words of love
and want and need
make me feel safe,
protected, less lonely.

It's these words
I hold on to
when you are not here.

When all I have is the
waiting and the longing.

Courtney Peppernell

as the time grows closer
the hearts beat more erra
                              tical
                                    ly
searching for the rhythm
of the other—
as if beating at the same time
is the key to teleportation(^)

thump thump zap

now we're in the same room
and texas doesn't seem so far
when the love in my heart
can take me to you
faster than a car
(or a plane or a train,
 or dammit *anything)*

your hair smells like lilacs
and you're wearing the shirt
i gave you last time
when you were afraid
your primal fear
would not let you sleep
without my scent near

i kiss you like your mouth is a lock
and my lips are the key

Zack Grey

if i turn the tumblers just right
you'll never again
be so far from me

thump thump zap

my hands are nearly empty
except a single strand of hair
it seems i haven't learned
my lesson yet

you were always and never
here and there

(i close my eyes again)
(my heart beats,
looking for yours)

thump thump zap

brown eyes smile at me
surrounded by
night-sky hair

ocean wave lips
curl &
break against my
boat dock mouth

you are so quiet in pain
but wordlessly your cries
pluck at the red string
connecting my heart and yours

Zack Grey

It catches up with me from time to time, the deep realization that you are not here. I'll be coming home from work, wanting to sit on my couch with you and drink a glass of wine, tell you about my day. But when I get home, you aren't there, and even if I wanted to call, I know you are already asleep.

there's an empty space
between my arm &
the sheets,
right where your
hips should be.

Zack Grey

Always a different time where you are. I've been living in all these other towns. I'm waking up to your sunset, calling your phone, hoping you aren't asleep. I just want to be there, with you, instead of being lonely all week.

if this dark world
keeps us apart
for many more nights,
promise me just one thing:

you will never stop
looking for my eyes
in the crowds of people
that pass you by.

Zack Grey

You are worlds away
in a time zone that
never makes any sense.

Why do I have to miss you
    like this,
buried in my pillow,
wishing it was you.

our twilight hearts
will find healing
in the light that
lives within
this darkness.

I tell myself every day that the distance doesn't matter, but lately I can't take it anymore. I want to wait forever, because every time you call, my heart stops, but it also breaks every time you walk out the door. In all these crowds, I am seeing your face, hearing your name in every empty space. I just want to come back home, and you'll be right there, waiting for me.

Courtney Peppernell

you are here,
but not;

even when your body
is far,
your soul never is.

Zack Grey

I have lost many things in my life: competitions, friends who didn't stay, a pair of shoes on a rainy day. I have lost love, because it was too hard, and dreams, because things got in the way. But every step, no matter how far, is a step closer to who you are.

darling, i'm praying to you—
the only goddess
i believe in.

keep the demons
away from my
light

with your arms
wrapped around me
tight.

pull the sleep
down over my eyes
so i can

dream of you tonight.

Zack Grey

Every other person
isn't you
and I'm tired of
pretending
being busy will do

because the truth is
no matter
how many seconds
I am distracted

I still just want
to be close to you

Courtney Peppernell

in art,
the empty places
are called
negative space,

but without you here,
the only emptiness
is inside me,
and everything surrounding it

is you
or things i
wish
were you.

Zack Grey

Grow Together / Grow Apart

They exist, those happy endings. A story of a girl who messages someone beautiful. All the messages, falling asleep with the screen still on, the phone calling as soon as she's home. Thousands of miles apart, plane ticket after plane ticket, the highs and the lows, the second-guessing, and finally the knowing. Then one day she's in an apartment, and the one she has loved despite the distance is lying asleep beside her, and the apartment is theirs.

Those happy endings do exist.

i've never been so happy
to be so sad

having you to miss
is a privilege

The reality is we are nearly always apart, but the magic is that we can love each other from miles away. I chose you because you made me want to live as deliberately as I could. You made me want to hold life in my hands and give it all I've got, no regrets, no what-ifs. Just you and me knowing that, despite all the obstacles in our way, we aren't falling apart.

she loved me so much
broken
that a single look
is all it took
to unbreak me
for her

Zack Grey

I am my own, always and first.
But when I am with you,
I am thinking about building
a life, a home.

you get me
so you get
me.

Our love exists inside a tiny seed, and it will grow if we promise to nurture and support its roots. If we can build a foundation together, then I know we can withstand every element, every season.

with you,

i feel that

most elusive thing:

happiness.

Zack Grey

But I love you in the way I love a clear sky, how I would build a bridge to walk to you, how I would drive all night just to be close to you. We didn't mean for it to turn out this way, but I wouldn't choose any other path, because I am in love with the way you exist, your eyes, your smile, your laugh.

Courtney Peppernell

i held on even when they
told me to let you go.

no, i wasn't surprised
when your hand
reached for mine.

love only smiles at us
when we're ready
to smile back.

Zack Grey

Maybe our love is too powerful
to be so close together

As though we are two magnets
connecting with such intensity
that if we touched
there'd be an explosion

Electric
Fiery

More than the universe
could withstand

Courtney Peppernell

you love me
through the pain
and i smile at you
through the ugly

Zack Grey

In the beginning, I would check the clock to see what time it was where you were. But now I know the time difference by heart. I wish those hours didn't exist, that instead they were just dreams in which we could meet. How I would tell you how safe you make me feel, even if every day I choose another hour to steal.

Courtney Peppernell

"i see you"

she says

but her eyes are

closed.

Zack Grey

We will dance through infinity with your hands in my hair and my legs wrapped around your waist. I will drown forever in the way you kiss me and breathe in your scent in every moment. There is a hole in my heart, the size of the ocean between us, but as far as the eye can see the sea is how much our love means to me.

it's saturday morning, and you were drinking with your friends last night. they slept over, because everyone around you feels at home in your presence, just like i do when i see your face. you love them too—a heart like yours cares more than it would like to admit.

it's 11am where you are, and i'm hundreds of miles away while you make a late breakfast for everyone fortunate enough to be so close to you.

i text you and tell you i miss you. you tell your friends to finish up because you have pressing business to attend to.

you're the kind of girl who gets invited to everything, and i'm the kind of boy who rarely accepts an invite,
but here we are, choosing each other—you spend hours on the phone with me when you could be with anyone, and i choose any moment i can spend with you over the company i always chose before: myself.

this saturday morning,
i'm on the phone at home with you.
i'm at home on the phone with you.

Zack Grey

We live on this earth together
we see the same moon
and pray to the same stars
and yet when you're watching the sunset
I'm watching the sunrise

Courtney Peppernell

today i saw the moon rise
in a sunny sky

this is the meeting of
day and night

a coming together
of you and me

Zack Grey

Our love is wrapped up in plane tickets and long-distance calls. Our hands reach between the sheets in the middle of the night, hoping for a body but feeling the empty space. A thousand miles seems so far, but this love I have for you grows by the hour.

We are two pieces of a puzzle, only the pieces are miles apart.

i'm thinking about my muscles
and how,
sometimes,
they give up on me when i am
tired of running.

& now,
i'm thinking of the moment when i see you
in the flesh for the first time—
will i collapse?

simply too tired
to hold myself together
when you are finally here to do it.

Zack Grey

I wake up to a text
        "I just wish you were here"
And I don't know what breaks my heart more,
the fact that, even if I wanted to,
I can't
or that lately it feels like we are always
destined to be apart.

Courtney Peppernell

i loved her
from a distance,
like an ancient
treasure
encased in glass.

and that's
how i learned
that some beautiful things
just aren't meant for me.

Zack Grey

I lost you
        even though you were miles away
And never really mine to lose
I still lost you

Courtney Peppernell

i miss me
more than
i miss you

But there have been many hands across my skin, and yet none have brought me more happiness then the sound of your voice in the early hours. Our hands have never met, our lips have never touched, our bodies have never entwined. But I love you with my heart and soul.

I do, I do.

Courtney Peppernell

Each time you leave, you take a piece of my heart with you. Lately, I am not sure how many more pieces can go before my heart is no longer whole.

we deserved our
moment in the sun
but you were
just too cold

Zack Grey

Sometimes I wonder, if we had both been in the same city, would it have been different? If every night you didn't have to miss me, would we still be together?

Courtney Peppernell

the world stops spinning
and we are expected to go on
as if the stillness
in our hearts
is not the death
of this love

Zack Grey

In the mirror, I begged myself not to get attached to you and your pretty eyes. But every time we met, you had to go back. If only I knew then what I know now, maybe I wouldn't have thought about you every minute, every hour. But I still love the way you made me feel, even if I never know when you're coming back. Darling, I am still so attached.

i can't eat today—
the hunger feels like
it's exactly where it belongs—
in this void
you left me with.

Zack Grey

Sometimes it feels like a curse, this love that keeps me alone. All the traveling back and forth and the career that keeps you in every other state but mine. Where do we go when the holidays don't seem like enough or the sale on plane tickets no longer excites me? What becomes of us when the loneliness is too much to handle and I'd rather be single than missing you so much?

Courtney Peppernell

i have a habit
of giving people
someone new to love
so they can leave me
behind

Zack Grey

I believe in a soul mate, someone who loves every corner, part, and inch of you, no matter how dark. I just never thought the universe would split my soul in half and cast the part I love most to the other side of the world.

Courtney Peppernell

This isn't easy, the constant leaving. Always feeling so alone, and we're both so afraid of the unknown. I'm sorry I'm all out of apologies, and there are just some things I don't know; I'm sorry I always have to come and go. Last night, in your apartment, over our last glass of wine and argument that lasted all day, I could see it in your eyes; you just want me to stay away.

Courtney Peppernell

i am restless, mind shriveled
and eaten alive by
giving love to a soul that
has never loved me quite as much.

i am empty. dead in
the darkness i live in
without having felt your
soft touch.

how is a man to keep loving
a soul tied to a body
that he cannot
be close to?

i am broken. how can i give up
when i will always remember
what it felt like to fall asleep
to your honeysuckle voice

but never kiss your lips?

i can't hold on any longer,
but i am too infected
to know if i must let go of
you or myself.

Zack Grey

When the sun rose, we were tangled limbs in bedsheets, skin on skin, hearts fused together. This memory plays on repeat, a record I can't escape. The way we tried to make time for each other, when we didn't have enough of it. And I know we tried to trust more and forget all the doubt, but once upon a time, when we felt lucky to have something so special it made saying goodbye so difficult, it became a burden and left us with the oldest story in the world: that some things just don't work out.

Courtney Peppernell

i'm afraid to
walk this
empty world
without you

They told us that sometimes home is not a place but a person, and yet with all this space between, home has become neither. There's no waiting on the front porch in the middle of winter with a hot chocolate and asking to watch movies until midnight. Instead, we both couldn't keep up with all the flights and the endless fighting.

Courtney Peppernell

if only the words
we write for each other
could bring us closer

maybe we would
share a kiss
in the same time zone

maybe you would laugh
in that way that kills me
and the sound of it
wouldn't be tainted by
phone static

maybe i'd stop feeling
like my heart was on
the other side of the world

and maybe the knives i stab you with
the claws you dig into my mind
twisting and turning all the time—

maybe we could
put our weapons away
and learn to heal the pain
instead of looking for ways
to feel again when
distance tries
to make our love
fade.

Zack Grey

All these affirmations online
reminding us that long distance
is for the bold.

We were bold, we were daring,
but the adventure still came to an end.

It doesn't mean I don't care anymore,
doesn't mean I'm any less bold.

But, darling, sometimes the distance
just isn't for everyone.

Courtney Peppernell

we can let this demolish us
like an old house
no longer lived in,

nothing but a memory
in the hearts of those
who once lived there,

or we can break like a bone—

there will be pain,
but we will grow back stronger
every time.

Zack Grey

I'm sorry we invested everything into a future that was always unplanned and a little hazy. I'm sorry we grew love out of false hope and made promises neither of us could keep. I still feel my heart beating to your ghost, imagining what your hands would feel like in my hair. I think about the map we made, dotted with cities we'd hold hands in, but neither of us ever boarded the plane. I'm sorry things became so vague and months of bliss turned into such regret. I will always wish we could have loved each other.

Courtney Peppernell

When I See You

This is the story of how the moon loved the sun. Even if their love was destined to be apart, until the moments they stole, with lips upon lips, breathing once more, during their eclipse.

this is an airport scene.
this time,
i'm not leaving alone.

Zack Grey

The first moment you walked through the arrival gate, the flowers I was holding seemed to glow brighter in response to your smile. The way you wrapped your arms around me, told me you knew I would be small, the way you smelled of lavender, and your voice didn't sound different at all. Then, walking back to my car, how your hand fit with mine, and we stepped in time. In the car, out of breath, filled with excitement, wonder, and relief. You said I needed to kiss you please, and I can't remember the rest, because my whole body was finally at ease.

Courtney Peppernell

they told me not to
get my hopes up,
that when you love someone
from the internet,
they're never what you expect.

they weren't wrong;
i never thought
someone could possibly be
greater than my
expectations.

Zack Grey

The way each chapter seems to end with your leaving, so between each sentence we make the most of the time we have. Like today, how we spent it in bed, holding each other and not thinking about when the chapter would end.

you're the only one
i've ever been
certain about.

Zack Grey

I remember the day we met as though it were yesterday. The way you handed me your heart, like a seed, and asked me to watch it grow. Now, that seed has flourished, and I've carved my initials into your skin. For every moment we are separated, people will know you're mine, and every moment we are together, we are reminded that our love is a love even the distance cannot deny.

Courtney Peppernell

what does
home
taste like?

—your lips.

"Are you still here?"
        I whispered through the dark.
"Yes."
You replied softly, surely.
And your hand found mine.
"I'm always here."

we went for a drive &
held hands the whole time.

it's unfair, the way you look at me
when i have to watch the road—

just know that my eyes
are drowning in you too.

Zack Grey

She's away for months, serving a purpose greater than yours or mine. It's impossible to explain the pride I feel for her, the ache in my chest each time she puts on that uniform and boards the ship. We tell each other to look at the moon every night, remember the way our hands dance across each other's spines; but when the nights are cloudy, I lie awake dreaming of the day her ship will finally come back home.

Courtney Peppernell

when the light turns red
your lips find mine

a brief moment
forever frozen
somewhere in time

Zack Grey

"I'll just stop by,"
        you always text, even if you are miles away.
But today, those miles don't exist.

you smell like

never say

goodbye

Zack Grey

It's always been
  your soul
  before your skin

It's always been
  your laugh
  before your touch

It's always been
  I miss you, I can't wait
  to see you again

Yet tonight
  as fate would permit
  you're in my arms
  and I am the happiest

Courtney Peppernell

you make the poet
forget how the words
fit together
when he feels your breath
on his neck

Zack Grey

I've played our bodies moving together over and over in my head, dreamt of the way you taste and the sounds you make as we unstitch ourselves thread by thread.

she calls me her
world
when she's
on top of me

—*on top of the world*

Zack Grey

And I've only experienced
a handful of Mondays by your side
But they're the best ones
I've ever had

I've only kissed you
a dozen times
But they're the most meaningful
my lips have ever tasted

I've only celebrated
one Christmas with your family
But it was enough to think
of them as my own

So few,
yet always mean so much

Courtney Peppernell

she opens her eyes in the dark
and still she sees me.

"you're real," she says.

"and yours," i say.

i can't see a damn thing,
but i know she's smiling,
just like i am.

Zack Grey

The sunlight fell through the parted curtain of the motel, tumbling over your open suitcase. You and I were wrapped in blankets, still too exhausted to move. We still had one more day, to just stay that way. Completely in love, unmoving, touching, just being, the suitcase unpacked.

Courtney Peppernell

"would you like to travel the world?"
she asked me.

i kissed her lips.
bit her ears.

trailed my
feather-tipped fingers

from her chest
to her toes.

"my love, i just did,"
i told her.

Zack Grey

My hands feel empty when they aren't exploring your skin, my lips feel empty when they aren't saying your name, my heart feels empty with every return ticket. Why must I spend all this time away from the person who makes me feel filled?

you were singing this morning,
with your mouth
closed.

the song of your heart
needs no
words.

The universe stole a glimpse into the world we live in and decided you and I should come together. Even if the moments are fleeting, even if they're tied up with weeks apart, the universe knows, somehow, we make each other better.

one day, i fell asleep
and never woke up.

i know this because
you were just a dream,

but now you are here.

i'm afraid to open my eyes.
what if you disappear?

Zack Grey

My soul is split,
from where I am
to where you are.

But tonight, it is whole again,
with you on the couch,
takeout on the table,
head on my shoulder,
watching movies with dim lights.

You're home again.

Courtney Peppernell

we catch each other
smiling like
i can't believe it,
how am i so lucky
to call you mine?

Zack Grey

Every love letter you've ever penned, I keep under my pillow, for all the cold nights alone, when without you my bed feels like a jail cell. But you'll never have to ask me twice if I believe in our love the way the moon believes in the night. Even in all the overthinking, even in all the distance, what matters are the moments you are here. What matters is my love for you just means so much.

Courtney Peppernell

what does it look like?
they ask me.

i could tell them that it
looks like a memory.
that it looks like
a midsummer porch
with ice-cold lemonade
in hand as cicadas cry
and the sun goes down.

like a wrong turn
in a city we've never been to,
talking to strangers on the street,
discovering places that feel like magic.

like you just fell asleep on my shoulder
when we have somewhere to be,
but you look so damn cute
with your eyes closed,
as if there's nothing left to look for
because you've already found it.

but when they ask me,
what does it look like?
i tell them it looks just like you.

—*love*

Zack Grey

When the nights become too difficult to bear, I remind myself how lucky I am to relearn you over and over again. Each time we part, we count down the moments until we are together once more, to learn all the things about each other we do adore. So, with you here, I will relearn the way your voice sounds in the morning; I will relearn the taste of your lips, the way your hair looks in the afternoon sunlight, the dimples down your spine, how your hand feels and fits in mine. Each time we meet, I will find all these new little things, always learning you, always teaching myself about your soul.

we must've said
"what is it?"
a thousand times each,

but we both knew what it was.

you were fighting
to keep your composure,
as was i.

that car ride
was one long goodbye.

Zack Grey

I just don't want you to forget me or forget what we have. I want you to see my reflection through the moonlight entering your window, I want you to feel my body as you wrap yourself in blankets, I want you to think of my smile in your coffee, I want you to picture all my favorite things as you walk down the street. I don't want our love wasted in empty sheets or replaced with another's breath. I want to be remembered in every moment lived.

Courtney Peppernell

your kiss was screaming:
i don't want to go,
but i have to.

it was enough,
knowing that you hurt
as much as i do.

Zack Grey

The last kiss before we part, I see galaxies with my eyes closed. I feel the heat of your skin, erupting, consuming, holding me in place. How can this moment have come so quickly again? A kiss to prove the waiting is worth it, a kiss to last the long winter once more.

Courtney Peppernell

you were still right there,
living,
breathing,
aching the same way i did.
but i had to let you go.

—*the hardest moment*

Zack Grey

In the beginning, it was so easy to show you the parts of me I wanted you to see. But you crawled under my skin and lit fires in the dust, and I am no longer a person with no hope but someone who loves you, like it's the last thing I will ever do. Like it's the last thing I will feel each and every time you leave.

Courtney Peppernell

crying never
felt so good

(i hope my tears
will always be
this happy)

Zack Grey

This is our story, long goodnights and static between calls. Wondering how much our hearts can take if another date drops out. I see your face in every horizon, your hair glowing red in each sunset, the freckles on your back every time you undress. I see you in baggage claim, with flowers and a smile. I'm finally home for a while, and I can't wait to hold you, my love, my home.

Courtney Peppernell

my feet are not
touching yours
how will i ever
sleep again?

Zack Grey

It's been six months, four hours, thirty-five minutes since you've slept in my bed, since I've kissed you, since I've held you. All this waiting, longing, hoping our two hearts won't split apart. Praying that all these complexities can one day be as simple as having morning coffee with you. But the moment you walk through the door, it's all worth it. When I see your face, dusty smile, and worn-out jeans, everything floods back. I can barely describe how it feels to have found the word "home" in you.

Courtney Peppernell

& the truck hits me:
tomorrow i will wake
to the rising sun
but the light will not
kiss my skin
the way you did

Zack Grey

The memory of that moment still lingers. How her lips tasted of honey and her hair felt soft in between my fingers. Now she's back home, and I'm burning cherry candles to forget her scent in my sheets. I'm closing my eyes, craving her heart beating against my chest, skin to skin, breath quickening. I'm binding my hands as they ache for every curve, every crackle, every part of her that lets me in. The memory exists, so it can be made over and over, each time her plane lands again.

Courtney Peppernell

and when i see you again
i will kiss you in a way
that makes the whole world
jealous of your lips

Zack Grey

But I don't want to wake up in an empty bed, with heavy arms from searching for you through the night. Is it so wrong for me to want your sun-drenched hair on the pillow next to mine, your sleepy morning smile in my line of sight, and your eyes shining back at me? Just stay a little longer, my love; just stay with me.

love stretches across the universe
the way a bridge stretches over water

my heart covers your sins
the way a sheet graces your body
in the cold of lonely night

and your body
tangles with mine
the way our souls tangle

across time

Zack Grey

My soul must have known yours since the beginning of time. Each life we have lived, finding each other, like two asteroids always colliding, unable to escape the other's pull. Every first meeting, always drunk with feeling and the familiar sense of *have we met before?* To this life now, always balancing on the edge of tomorrow, always one step closer to where you are. These boundaries do not exist between love and space and time, because even in the moments I have to wait for you, I know in every other life you'll always be mine.

Courtney Peppernell

i have spent the last 120 hours with you
right in front of my eyes. right where
my hands can reach and feel
the softness of your skin.
i have spent the last 120 hours
with my lips never more than a few feet away
from kissing yours.
i have spent the last 120 hours
dreading this moment.
the feeling grows familiar yet worse.
we're shamelessly letting tears fall
in front of hundreds of people
who just want to get through security
and go wherever it is the plane will take them.
one last embrace, one last "it's going to be okay,"
and you're in a quick-moving line
while i go down the escalator, still crying.
more than a younger me ever thought
a grown man should.
this short walk back to my car is the
longest of my life, and the 90-minute
drive home feels like 90 years.
what i mean to tell you is this:
for you, every tear is worth it.
for you, i'd drive a million more lonely hours.
for you, every night spent alone
is worth waiting for the few
when you'll be right next to me.

Zack Grey

the soul?
of course it can leave the body.

how else could we have
entwined
moments after meeting

if our spirits were not
two pieces
rejoining?

Zack Grey

She asked me once what would I do if she lost her memory. How would I remind her of my touch, my scent, the way we kiss, from all these miles away.

And so I told her, "You can still feel the sunlight from thousands of light-years away, you can still see the beauty in the stars burning miles and miles before yesterday, you can still hear the call of your love's voice even after the dream ends, you can still understand the magic of a letter long after the words have been penned."

I told her that memory is more than being present. It is in the way I feel every time I see a flower in her favorite color; it is in the playlist we made each other this past summer. It is in the stories we share about our day; it is in the pictures we have that will last forever.

I told my love, "The space between us is not measured by how many lonely nights we spend apart but rather all the beautiful moments always connecting my heart to your heart."

Courtney Peppernell

for now . . .

this is goodbye.
sorry,
not goodbye.
i've never liked that word.
see you soon.

for now,
you are there and i am here.
i'm jealous of the people
who get to see you every day.
i am jealous of the people
who take your scent for granted.
i am jealous of the people
who get to touch your hand,
even if only for an instant.

for now,
my lips ache,
remembering the way you taste.
my body wonders when it will
fit so perfectly beside you again.
my hands miss the feeling
of your fingers lacing with mine.

for now,
i will probably cry
every time you leave,
just like i did the first time.

it hurts not knowing
when i'll see you again.

for now,
i will wake up every morning,
reach to the other side of the bed,
and find that you are not there.

for now, i will tell you
that i miss you
every single day,
but not as often as i feel it
(which is all the time).

for now,
i will spend all the time
that i'd rather spend with you
working on me,
so when i see you the next time,
you will smile even more,
knowing that i am the best i can be.

for now . . .
i will hold your hand,
i will kiss you,
i will connect
the constellation on your face
with my finger,
but only in my dreams.

Thank you for reading this book.

We hope you enjoyed reading it as much as we enjoyed writing it. Feel free to write to us at courtney@pepperbooks.org and zackgreywrites@gmail.com, or follow along with our journeys on Instagram @courtneypeppernell and @zackgreywrites.

Andrews McMeel Publishing
a division of Andrews McMeel Universal
1130 Walnut Street, Kansas City, Missouri 64106

www.andrewsmcmeel.com

20 21 22 23 24 BVG 10 9 8 7 6 5 4 3 2 1

ISBN: 978-1-5248-5827-8

Library of Congress Control Number: 2020936518

Illustrations by Justin Estcourt

Editor: Patty Rice
Art Director/Designer: Diane Marsh
Production Editor: Elizabeth A. Garcia
Production Manager: Cliff Koehler